# MARPLE
# RAIL TR

GW01459041

Two guided Trails to locations of
railway historic interest in Marple and District
for the walker, cyclist and motorist.

Profusely illustrated

by
Warwick R. Burton M.A. (Cantab)

Published by
M.T. & W.R. Burton
Marple

# Contents:

# Abbreviations:

| | |
|---|---|
| G.C. | Great Central Railway |
| G.C. & Mid. | Great Central and Midland Joint Railway |
| G.C. & N.S. | Great Central and North Staffordshire Joint Railway |
| L.N.W. | London and North Western Railway |
| M.S.L. | Manchester, Sheffield and Lincolnshire Railway |

# Acknowledgements:

A great many people have contributed towards the information contained in this booklet; too many to name individually. But I must acknowledge my debt to the late "Hughie" Fletcher, who passed on to me a lifetime's knowledge of Marple's railways derived from a railway career beginning on the Midland Railway. I owe a great deal to my parents who have encouraged me in writing this book, and first gave me the love of walking, which prompted me to explore Marple's countryside and railway sites.

I am indebted to all the authors referred to in the bibliography; to Dr. C.T.G. Boucher and E. Oldham for information on the Canal and Tramway; to members of Marple Antiquarian Society for information and encouragement; and to many members of railway staff for assistance and reminiscenses.

Particular thanks for photographs are due to I.R. Smith, E. Oldham, H.C. Casserley, R. Gee, J.R. Hillier and R. Keeley, who have all supplied me with first class prints. Specific credits accompany each photograph in the text, photographs taken by the author are so credited; photographs with no credit are from negatives in the author's collection.

I wish to thank all those who have pointed out errors and omissions in my first book "The Railways of Marple and District from 1794". I would appeal to all who read this book to do the same.

*Cover photo: L.M.S. Class 5 M.T. 4.6.0 (Black five) heads the 1530 Manchester Central to Sheffield Midland over Marple Goyt Viaduct in June 1966.*

# Introduction:

Marple is an area rich in industrial archaeology: within the former Urban District of Marple are two Canals with an aqueduct and lock flight; remains of kilns and watermills; surviving mills from the 19th century heyday of 'King Cotton'; and remains of coal mines and tramways. Four railways are still in use, with four open stations, and there are the remains of one closed line and two closed stations.

It is on the railway aspect of industrial archaeology that this book concentrates, and is designed to guide you to the locations of railway interest in Marple by the most scenic and rewarding route, along with some background information.

Two Rail Trails are suggested, passing through countryside which is extremely beautiful and peaceful, including stretches along river bank and canal towpath, or through woods, delighting even those with no interest in railways. So the Trails in this book are recommended for the whole family. The scars of the Industrial Revolution have mellowed into a mature, picturesque landscape in Marple, and in many places the scenery is enhanced by the fine engineering of the canal and railway age.

This book is also a sequel to my earlier work "The Railways of Marple and District from 1794", and contains some material and photographs which could not be included in the first work due to lack of space. In particular it describes the appearance of the stations and lines, in use and closed, as they were in 1982.

Two Trails are suggested. The first, covering the Marple Viaducts, Canal and Marple Bridge, is the more picturesque, and is recommended to those who do not know the area, or only have limited time. The second is more adventurous, in terms of distance and difficulty of terrain; the locations of rail interest are also more spread out. The two Trails do not overlap except that the last 1½ miles of both coincide.

The Trails start and finish at Marple or Rose Hill stations, where there is ample car parking. Marple residents can of course start at any convenient point. Distances are given for the length of each Trail. There are a number of deviations off the main Trails to additional points of interest; these are indicated as deviations in the text, and are not included in the distances given.

Distances are given for the walker, cyclist and motorist. The walker will gain most from the Trails, as he will pass many items of interest not accessible by car; the cyclist and motorist, will have to keep parking and walking to see most of the locations. Though deviations have been suggested for the cyclist and motorist to avoid paths and tracks impassible by vehicles, the Trails still include some rather rough tracks. All the main locations visited are numbered and these numbers are shown on the map of the district at the front of the book, which is designed to guide you round the Trails. All locations are also given a 6 figure grid reference to pinpoint them on the Ordnance Survey Map, which would also be useful in following the Trails.

69 Bowden Lane,
Marple,
Cheshire.
February, 1982

First Published: May 1982.

Marple Station in its late 19th century heyday, c 1890, looking towards Manchester. Note that Marple North Signalbox is just visible under the bridge beyond the station, and the "knob up" ground frame cabin serving the goods yard can be seen under the right side of the footbridge linking the two main platforms.

A horse drawn landau outside Marple Station on Brabyns Brow cab rank c 1900.

# TRAIL 1
## Marple Viaducts, Canal, "Roman" Lakes and Marple Bridge

Starts and finishes : Marple Station.
Distance : 4½ miles.
Walking conditions : Good.
Cycling/Motoring conditions : A lot of rough tracks.
Refreshments : Pub food in Marple and Marple Bridge.
Cafes at Roman Lakes and Marple Bridge.

*A moderate Trail, ideal for all the family, passing through very picturesque scenery. Ought to be walked if at all possible.*

The Trail starts at (1) MARPLE STATION, (SJ963894), opened in 1865 on the single track Marple, New Mills and Hayfield Junction Railway. The line was doubled in 1866 and taken over by the M.S.L. and Midland Railways Jointly in 1869, and a goods yard opened. It was substantially rebuilt in 1875 with 4 platforms and a huge array of canopies and buildings. At the grouping it was G.C. & Mid Joint and in 1923 it became L.M.S. and L.N.E.R. The station lost its goods yard in 1964, and was demolished and rebuilt as it now stands in 1970.

The station is best viewed from the south from Brabyns Brow overbridge. Of the original station only the platforms survive, now raised in height, and the 1875 footbridge. Taking the Down side first, on your left, the platform of 1865 lengthened in 1875 survives, but shortened at the Southern end. The large rough grassy area up against the retaining wall of the bridge is the site of the large range of 1865 buildings; the site of the street entrance to the stair hall can be made out in the blocking of the gap with new stonework to the left of the bridge near the telephone kiosk. High on the

*Steam age commuter rush hour operating at Marple on 20th September 1958. On the left L.N.E.R. L.1 2.6.4.T 67751 calls on the 1729 Manchester London Road - Hayfield, while on the right ex G.C. A.5 4.6.2T 69801 waits to run round in the Up loop after terminating with the 1700 ex London Road. Note the water column, and the wooden goods shed behind the loop. (R. Keeley).*

5

embankment side can be seen the 3 brick abutments which supported the water tank feeding the station's 3 water columns. The site of the Down bay platform 1 is concealed in the undergrowth beind the waiting rooms, and is partly filled in; its northern end can however be seen at the top end of the Down platform, where the foundations of the 2 water columns - one for Down main and one for the bay platform - can also be seen.

On the Up side, on your right, the platform of 1875 survives, but to only half its original width. The line of the right hand wall of the booking office buildings indicates the original width of the platform, which was an island with a loop platform behind. The 1981 colour light signal stands on the exact site of its 19th century semaphore predecessor. Steps now lead down from the road to the station car park. The entrance to these steps used to lead to a 140 foot long footbridge to the Up platform which straddled the line to the loop platform, and also a 45 foot turntable: this was situated where the Permanent Way Department huts and present staircase now are. You can still see the massive wooden stopblocks of the Turntable line, and of the adjoining siding which passed through the large wooden goods warehouse, which was in the centre of what is now the car park. On the far right is the massive retaining wall of St. Martin's churchyard, against which ran two coal sidings.

Descend to the Up platform, pass through the booking hall, and continue along the Up platform passing a gap in the fence where the 1905 signalbox stood prior to resignalling in 1981. Behind you can see the former width of the Up platform and the site of the Up Loop platform 4, and mile post 176¾ from London (St Pancras), via Millers Dale and Derby (a line now closed). Beyond is a disused portion of the old, lower platform where the site of the Up loop and two shunt necks can be seen.

Now return to Brabyns Brow Bridge, cross the road and look over the parapet southwards. To the left can be seen the large hollow carved out, to house (2) THE TURNTABLE (SJ963893) of 50 feet installed in 1898 to replace the one in the goods yard. To the right can be seen the stone-lined recess which housed Marple South Signalbox closed in 1905. Along the cutting side to the left or east of the line ran the private footpath from "Beechwood", the residence of Edward Ross, the Secretary of the M.S.L.

*The latter days of steam at Marple. B.R. Standard Class 5 4.6.0 heads a train of empty stock for a return Belle Vue - West Riding excursion on Easter Monday 1967. These locomotive were common on the line in the mid 1950's when they used to appear on local "running in" turns when brand new from Derby. Note the site of the Up loop platform 4 (left) and Down bay platform 1 (right) at the north end of the station. (I.R. Smith).*

*Steam age freight at Marple in 1964. An Up Goods Train of coal empties enters the north end of the station behind a Fowler 4F 0.6.0 43967 built by the Midland Railway at Derby. Note the water column on the Down main platform and the line of the Down bay. (J.R. Hillier).*

Now recross the road and take the narrow footpath "Seven Stiles" first left of the telephone box. This gives a good view of the piers of the water tank, and a little further on can be seen the grilles covering the channels taking water to the columns at the north end of the station. Passing through a wicket gate, do not follow the path as it veers left, but carry straight on until you come to (3) BRABYNS PARK OVERBRIDGE (SJ 963895) of 1865. From here there is an excellent view of the station and the abandoned bay and loop platforms. Looking the other way, there is a good view of (4) MARPLE NORTH TUNNEL (SJ962897) emerging from under the canal and 99 yards long. To the right, up against the bridge you are standing on, observe the stone-lined recess of Marple North Signalbox also closed in 1905. Over the bridge just into the Park, and about 2 feet east of the retaining wall or railway fence can be seen iron markers bearing the letters "G.C. & M" stamped on them marking the actual limit of railway ownership.

Recross the bridge and follow the old coach road uphill for about 100 yards, until you see a flight of stone steps on your right. Climb these to reach (5) THE PEAK FOREST CANAL. The motorist or cyclist will however have to return to the road, ascend Brabyns Brow, and take the minor road first right after crossing the canal to reach this point. The Canal was promoted in 1794 by Samuel Oldknow and others to convey lime from the Peak District and service his Mellor Mill. Engineered by Benjamin Outram, it was completed in 1804, but passed into the M.S.L. in 1845. Follow the canal towpath downward along the flight of locks, of which there are 16 in all. (The motorist however will have to follow the road). Two locks on, note the railway passing under the canal by means of Marple North Tunnel. Three locks beyond this you may detect a shelf like hollow and wharf on the far side of the canal, which is the site of the old Marple Wharf rail/canal transhipment siding, of which more anon.

Eventually (6) MARPLE VIADUCT (SJ 955902) comes into view. A skew bridge at its southern end crosses over the canal which so recently passed over the railway at Marple North Tunnel - such is the rate of descent of the locks. Walk out onto (7) MARPLE AQUEDUCT (SJ 955901) of 1804 to admire Marple Viaduct of 1863, with its 12 noble

*The demolition of Marple's goods shed after closure to freight on 5th October, 1964. Note the massive timbers of this shed, constructed in c.1875. The site is now occupied by the car park.*

stone arches, 124 feet above the river at its highest point and 918 feet long. Note the fine "rusticated" masonry, disfigured by patches of blue brick, used to patch the structure as an economy measure in the 1940's. The works beside the Aqueduct are on the site of the former "Aqueduct Hotel" built to refresh those using the canal. A good view of Marple Viaduct and Aqueduct may be obtained by an extension to the Trail: carry on across the Aqueduct, follow the canal to the first overbridge, (Near which is the site of the temporary Compstall Station, closed in 1865), and just beyond this turn left and double back along the edge of the wood until after a couple of hundred yards you come to the viewpoint.

Now return the way you came along the Aqueduct to the first canal overbridge. From here follow the road along the right or west side of the canal. This road is on the course of (8) THE MARPLE TRAMWAY (SJ 957900 to 963882) built to link the upper and lower canal levels, and to carry construction materials. It was authorised in 1797, opened by 1800, doubled in 1801, closed in 1807 when the canal was fully operational, and lifted in 1816. It ran 1½ miles from the canal on the far, Romiley, side of the River Goyt, crossing the valley on a temporary viaduct, and along the course of the canal under construction to the Lime Kilns (16). The Tramway was said to be a self acting incline with descending loaded wagons hauling empties up, but in view of the slight gradients over much of its length, this probably refers to inclines crossing the Goyt Valley; Horse traction was almost certainly used on the more level sections. The rails employed were similar to those of the Peak Forest Tramway at Bugsworth, with "L" shaped plate rails and trucks with detachable bodies.

Before you get more than a few yards up the road climb a path up the bank to your right, to view (9) MARPLE WHARF JUNCTION (SJ 957900) so named after the 1862 Marple Wharf Branch (10) which here diverged from the main line. Later in 1869, the Macclesfield, Bollington and Marple Railway joined up here as well. This was later G.C. & N.S. Joint, was terminated at Rose Hill in 1970 and 'singled' in 1981, when Marple Wharf Signalbox was closed and removed by the Peak Railway Society for preservation. In these days of terrorist attacks, it is interesting to note that in 1916 a Sinn Fein extremist attempted to shoot the signalman at Marple Wharf Junction, John Axon of Oakwood. In the event he escaped with injuries. Later in 1921 the Sinn Fein tried unsuccessfully to blow up the signalbox.

8

Carry on up the road, and before you have travelled far you will observe a large gap in the embankment to your right. This is the course of (10) the short MARPLE WHARF BRANCH (SJ 958898). After the crossing it led to high and low level wharfs beside the canal; the southern two sidings were below canal level, with a loading bank between wagons and canal basin. Note the massive stone blocks edging this loading bank, now toppled by the roots of trees. The discerning eye can also pick out the rotting remains of sleepers and rusty ironwork, despite the branch having closed in c.1900.

A little further on, the road passes over the north portal of Marple North Tunnel, giving a good view of the line. Now continue along the road and course of the tramway for about ½ mile to Station Road. Just before the road in a field to the right can be seen the earthworks of (11) LEY HEY PARK TRAMWAY (SJ 962893) a narrow gauge line used c.1880 in the construction of the adjoining estate by the contractor Enoch Tempest. On reaching Station Road cross over, noting the stone house to the right which was the office of the Peak Forest Canal Company, and enter (12) ST MARTIN'S ROAD (SJ 963892) to the left of the canal. This was laid out largely along the line of the canal tramway, and after its closure became a toll road. Immediately on your right is a small brick hut which housed the meter controlling the water from the canal to supply the station water columns, and enabled the M.S.L., and later G.C. who owned the canal, to charge the Midland Railway who used the columns, for the water consumed. Passing the Canal Wharf and Samuel Oldknow's warehouse, (to house goods to and from Mellor Mill), now tastefully converted into offices, turn right to cross the canal by the small bridge of Lock 10. On either side of the canal to the north of the bridge can be seen slots in the coping, for the cast iron girders of the bridge where the Marple Tramway left the course of St Martin's Road and crossed the Canal.

Return to St Martin's Road, turn right and follow it, (passing the toll house on the right), to Oldknow Road. Straight ahead in the recreation ground is (13) an EMBANKMENT OF THE MARPLE TRAMWAY (SJ 963887) curving away towards the Limekilns.

Turn right up Oldknow Road and cross the canal by (14) POSSETT BRIDGE (SJ 962887) said to be named after the quantities of the drink of that name consumed during its construction. See if you can spot the date of completion - October, 18th 1804.

*The "Harwich Boat Train" (1516 Manchester Piccadilly to Harwich Parkeston Quay) heads south through Marple on the 7th October, 1978. The station is largely as it is now except for the introduction of colour light signalling and demolition of the signalbox. (Author)*

*Marple Signalbox on the 12th September 1978 shortly before closure in July 1980. Built in 1905 to standard Midland design, with horizontal boarding on the lower storey, vertical boarding on the upper, sliding windows with cut-off top corners, a low pitched slate roof and 'Gothic' finials (Author).*

Descend by steps to your right to the canal to inspect the bridge with its two arches; the left hand one led to a now filled in branch which replaced the Marple Tramway as access to the Limekilns. There was another branch on the right to Hollins Mill, its position visible in a change of edging to the canal. This area was landscaped by the Marple Civic Society in 1966, as part of Operation Springclean, and visited by the Queen in 1968.

Follow the canal upward via the fine horse tunnel, with its complicated side passages, to reach, after more locks, (15) TOP LOCK (SJ962885) where the 1826 Macclesfield canal joins. There is a fine roving bridge here, a toll house adjoining, and another fine warehouse. The handsome stone house opposite Top Lock was the premises of Jink's Boatyard. Return a few yards down the canal, and take a narrow track to the right over the first canal bridge, and you reach (16) the LIMEKILNS built 1797 - 1800 by Samuel Oldknow. Lime was charged into these from barges on the canal above and when processed removed by tramway. Originally the lime was conveyed by the Marple Tramway, which started here, to the canal beyond the Aqueduct; after the completion of the locks, the tramway led to a warehouse with a rounded end (still existing) on the south or right of the site for distribution by cart, and to a boathouse for discharge into barges on the canal branch. The boathouse also survives, on the left of the site, its arched docks converted into rooms of a house. There was also an inclined tramway up to the level of the canal above.

Turn right out of the Limekilns, then almost immediately left (at a fork junction) down Arkwright Road to a crossroads. Turn right down Faywood Drive, noting the B.R. signs to Marple and Rose Hill Stations, designed to direct trippers from the Roman Lakes. The road forks almost immediately - take the left hand fork, passing (17) "BEECHWOOD" (SJ965887) a large Victorian Mansion built over Marple South Tunnel. This was the residence of Edward Ross, J.P., Secretary of the M.S.L. from 1850, to his death in 1892. Note particularly the little iron footbridge crossing to what was a garden; this bridge was said to be to allow the family's children to enter the garden without coming into contact with low-class children!

10

*"Beechwood", the residence of Edward Ross, Secretary of the M.S.L. from the north. Note the footbridge to connect the garden above Marple South Tunnel. 12th September 1978. (Author).*

*The interior of Marple Wharf Junction Signalbox shortly before closure in July 1980.*

Descend the long straight road down into the Goyt Valley, noting the fine view of the line on its ledge above the river. A footbridge can be seen crossing the line. This is (18) "ARKWRIGHT'S BRIDGE" (SJ 966883) built to carry the footpath used by apprentices from Mellor Mill below to reach All Saints Church on Sundays, and so named after Oldknow's better known partner. At the bottom of the incline, on the right beside the river, stood Marple Lodge. If there does not appear to be room for a house here, this is not surprising as in 1893 the embankment of the railway collapsed carrying away the Up line and half burying Marple Lodge in the avalanche: and that was the end of Marple Lodge.

The more energetic may care to deviate at this point and take a zig zag path up the hillside to view "Arkwright's Bridge" (Bridge 24) at close quarters - whence there is a good view of (19) MARPLE SOUTH TUNNEL (SJ 965887) 224 yards long. If you use the path you will pass a small arched dummy viaduct, Bridge 24A, built to support the embankment where the slip occurred.

*New and old steam locomotives meet at Marple Wharf Junction in August 1956. An Up train of coal empties is hauled by a wartime "Austerity" 8F 2.8.0, while a pre first world war L.N.W. "Bowen-Cooke" Class 7F.0.8.0 No 49093 stands at the Home signal. Note the fine Midland Railway lower quadrant signals (E. Oldham).*

12

*B.R. Standard "Britannia" Class 7 4.6.2 express locomotive No. 70013 "Oliver Cromwell" heads the Midland Main Line Centenary Railtour northwards through Marple Wharf Junction on June 8th 1968. This type of locomotive regularly hauled the London St Pancras - Manchester Central expresses through Marple in the late 1950's and early 1960's on Sunday diversions off the usual Disley Tunnel Route. The signal box was erected by the L.M.S. in 1927 but is of Midland design. Note the milepost 177¼ from London St Pancras on the box. (I.R. Smith).*

The main Trail now crosses the River Goyt, passing on the right the site of Oldknow's residence of Mellor Lodge, and through the area of (20) MELLOR MILL (SJ 967884), built in 1790 as a calico and muslin mill and burnt down in 1892; the impressive remains of the wheel pits and subterranean water leats can still be seen. The stone date tablet of the mill is preserved in the memorial park, Marple. The track forks-turn right and follow this, past the drained millpond on the left, to (21) BOTTOMS HALL (SJ 969882) where the apprentices who worked at Mellor Mill were housed. There turn right and follow the track alongside (22) the "ROMAN LAKES" (SJ 969879) which are in fact the mill-pond and leats of Mellor Mill, converted into a boating and fishing lake after the demise of the Mill in 1892. In years gone by Marple Station was hard pressed to deal with the excursion traffic of day trippers to the lakes. From the valley bottom there is a fine view of (23) MARPLE GOYT VIADUCT (SJ 968876) thrown across the Goyt Valley at its narrowest point where the glacial moraine of Strawberry Hill almost blocks the valley. The Viaduct built in 1865 is a fine seven arch stone structure, with a wide girder span across the river itself. A fine view of the viaduct may be obtained by continuing 200 yards along the track, passing the Milldam weir, and Attendant's House (later Webb's Tea Rooms for the benefit of railway excursionists), and ascending a path on the left.

Now retrace your steps to the site of Mellor Mill and bear right for Marple Bridge, instead of back to the Goyt. This track is passable by cars but is very rough! From this track, at the crest of the hill, there is a fine view across the valley of "Beechwood" perched on a cliff (like nearly every railway location in Marple).

Arriving in Marple Bridge, you reach the main road, Town Street. The motorist would do well to park in one of the car parks here. Just up the road to the right you may like to look at an 18th century water powered spade forge, with surviving iron breast wheel. Now climb up Hollins Lane opposite the track from the roman Lakes to reach (24) ST MARY'S CHURCH (Roman Catholic) (SJ 9966893) where Edward Ross, the Secretary of the M.S.L., worshipped and which he beautified with various gifts. His prominent

*L.N.W. "Bowen-Cooke" 7F. 0.8.0 No 49093 gets the road through Marple Wharf Junction with a Down coal train in August 1956. Note the Macclesfield line joining from the right (E. Oldham)*

monument is to be seen in the Churchyard beyond the Church and up the hill towards the top. Now return to Marple Bridge, and turn right into Town Street. Almost immediately on your right is (25) the "ROYAL SCOT" HOTEL (SJ 965894), which has been so renamed quite recently, having been the "Railway" since as early as 1833. Note the pair of locomotive handlamps beside the door. Further on turn left to cross the Goyt past (26) THE MIDLAND HOTEL (SJ 964895) a reminder of that great Company's presence in Marple. Opposite the "Midland" are the cottages into whose sunken gardens a railway horse drawn delivery lorry and horses driven by a carter called "Old Yarwood" were flung by a runaway motor lorry just after the 1st World War. These cottages stand at the gate of Brabyns Hall (now demolished) whose owners the Hudsons, were so opposed to the building of the railway; (27) ST MARTIN'S CHURCH (SJ 963894) which you pass on Brabyns Brow, was built by them in 1870, reputedly to forestall any expansion of the station. Beside the lych gate of the church observe the small arched gateway leading to a path between the station and church yard, which is where "Seven Stiles" footpath used to emerge onto Brabyns Brow, before it was diverted in 1875 to run west of the station. Opposite the church is the site of a cattle market, now a car park, which for many years brought much livestock traffic to the station. And so back to Marple Station where the Trail began.

*Preserved Steam in action. L.N.E.R. A4 4.6.2 streamlined Pacific No 4498 "Sir Nigel Gresley" on a Railtour from Manchester to Scarborough via Sheffield on Saturday 29th April 1978. Taken from Arkwright's Bridge just south of Marple South Tunnel. The locomotive is named after the designer Sir Nigel Gresley, C.M.E. of the G.N.R. and later L.N.E.R. 1911 - 1941 (I.R. Smith).*

*Midland Compound 4.4.0 No 41048 heads Up Derby Local composed of miscellaneous stock near Strines 1954 (E. Oldham).*

*Ex G.C. Mixed Traffic J.11 No 64441 enters Rose Hill with a Macclesfield train just after nationalisation c.1951. (R. Gee).*

# TRAIL 2
## Rose Hill, High Lane, Middlewood, Disley Tunnel, Strines, Marple Bridge

| | | |
|---|---|---|
| Starts | : | Rose Hill Station. |
| Finishes | : | Marple Station. |
| Distance - Walker | : | 10 miles, |
| Motorist/Cyclist | : | 18 miles |
| Refreshments | : | 3 pubs with food and cafes in High Lane; cafe at Roman Lakes; Pubs, cafe and restaurant in Marple Bridge. |
| Walking conditions | : | Rough and muddy in places. |
| Cycling/Motorist conditions | : | Some rough tracks. |

*A longish circular Trail, with some distance between the locations of railway interest. Scenery pleasant, improving as Trail progresses. Most likely to appeal to hiker or person interested in railways. Overlaps with Trail 1 for locations 20 - 27.*

The Trail begins at (28) ROSE HILL STATION (SJ 950887) opened by the Macclesfield, Bollington and Marple Railway in 1869 on a single line, doubled in 1871. The line was taken over jointly by the M.S.L. and North Staffordshire Railway (later G.C. & N.S.) The station layout is clearly visible from the Stockport Road overbridge to the North. The site of the 3 road goods yard, closed in 1965, is now occupied by a car park and bus/rail interchange. The line beyond to Macclesfield was closed in 1970, though the branch to Rose Hill remained double with both station platforms in use until 1980. On the left the disused Up platform is devoid of buildings, though the filled in recess where the main buildings stood is quite easily perceived. A little further along the platform is another such filled in recess which probably held the station's original signal box, before it was replaced in c 1900 by one at the south end of the Down platform. The Down platform on the right retains its buildings, which house a ticket office in the former Ladies Waiting Room, and a staff mess room and waiting room in the former Booking Office. The former ticket office was housed in a tiny lean to shed south of the main building; this was in addition to the main ticket office on the Up platform. Right down at the far end of the car park is Bowden's Coal Yard, all that remains of a once flourishing railbourne trade. Access to the car park and the bus stop is from the road leading to the S.M.B.C. Council Depot, where formerly Marple U.D.C. had a private siding, and is on

*Rose Hill Station from the North in 1962. The original 1870 buildings are on the left. Note the N.S. style signalbox, and the Marple U.D.C. Private siding disappearing behind it. The goods yard is quite busy with at least 5 coal wagons, and 2 vans of general merchandise (Mowat Collection).*

the site of the rail served Tym's Brickworks. Outside the station is a public house, once known as the "Gun Inn" but rebuilt and renamed the "Railway Hotel" with the opening of the line. The Inn sign depicts L.M.S. Class 5 express locomotive No 5552 "Silver Jubilee", a type never seen on the line!

The walker should now follow the course of the old line southward. After about a mile, just before Torkington Bridge, the post of Rose Hill's Down Distant signal lurches drunkenly; near here a train was snowed up in the 1947 winter. Further on, just beyond where the pylons join the trackbed, and opposite a massive rectangular spoil heap from

*A train and ex G.C. C.13 4.4.2T locomotive snowed up near Torkington Lane between Rose Hill and High Lane in the 1947 winter.*

18

*Rose Hill station as it was on 12th September 1978 prior to singling in 1980. A d.m.u. waits at the Down departure platform for Manchester. Since this photograph was taken the Up line (right) has been lifted. Note the site of the lean-to booking office showing in the brickwork of the building. (Author).*

Disley Tunnel, turn right off the trackbed down a farm track, and turn left to view (29) DISLEY TUNNEL WEST PORTAL (SJ 943862). The cyclist and motorist however will have to go via Stockport Road, Hibbert Lane (passing the gigantic Goyt Cotton Spinning Mill of 1905), and Hawk Green onto Windlehurst Road; leave this road at the bottom of the hill after crossing the canal and turn right into Torkington Lane; bear left off this lane, shortly after crossing the course of the Macclesfield line, into Threaphurst Lane. Disley Tunnel at 2 miles 346 yards is the 6th longest in Britain; it was completed in 1901 on the Midland Railway's "New Line" opened in 1902, to by-pass Marple Station and Stockport and give a fast route to Manchester. It was closed as an express route in 1968, and is now only open for company freight trains from the Peak District to I.C.I. works in Cheshire. At this point a contractors line diverged from the Macclesfield line, whose embankment can be seen above the tunnel, for conveyance of materials for the construction of the tunnel: no trace of it however remains. Note also the Midland Railway worker's cottages nearby.

The walker should now rejoin the trackbed by means of a track through a gate opposite the cottages, and carry on south to the site of High Lane Station. The cyclist or motorist should continue south along Threaphurst Lane until it joins the A.6. Turn left and after a few hundred yards you will reach (30) HIGH LANE STATION (SJ 944856). The station, closed in 1970, was very similar to Rose Hill, except it had no goods yard. Now only the bare and ruinous platforms are visible, but the foundations of the Main Up buildings and small wooden waiting room/booking office on the Down side can be found amid the undergrowth. Note that the A6 road bridge over the course of the railway has recently been largely filled in, except for a tunnel for a bridleway, to take the pounding of modern traffic. To the east of the station is the site of a colliery closed before the railway came.

From High Lane Station it is only a short ½ mile walk southward to (31) MIDDLEWOOD STATIONS (SJ 946848). The cyclist or motorist should return west down the A6 and ½ mile along take the first left, a minor lane, and continue through the woods, crossing the L.N.W. Buxton line by Norbury Crossing. After ¾ mile you will crest

*Ex G.C. C13 4.4.2T No. 67426 arrives at High Lane with an Up Local on the 4th September 1954. Note the immaculate gardens. (H.C. Casserley).*

the brow of a hill and see on the left a sign for the station, reached by a footpath: you will have to walk from here. There were two stations here, Higher and Lower, with no road access, but approached by at least four different footpaths through the woods. The Lower station is on the Stockport, Disley and Whaley Bridge Railway of 1857, later taken over by the L.N.W. The Higher station was opened in 1879 to provide interchange facilities, though the two stations remained seperately run until Nationalisation. The Low Level Station, retains buildings, consisting of Ticket Office and Waiting Room, on the Down side only, with a "bus shelter" on the Up on the site of the original principal

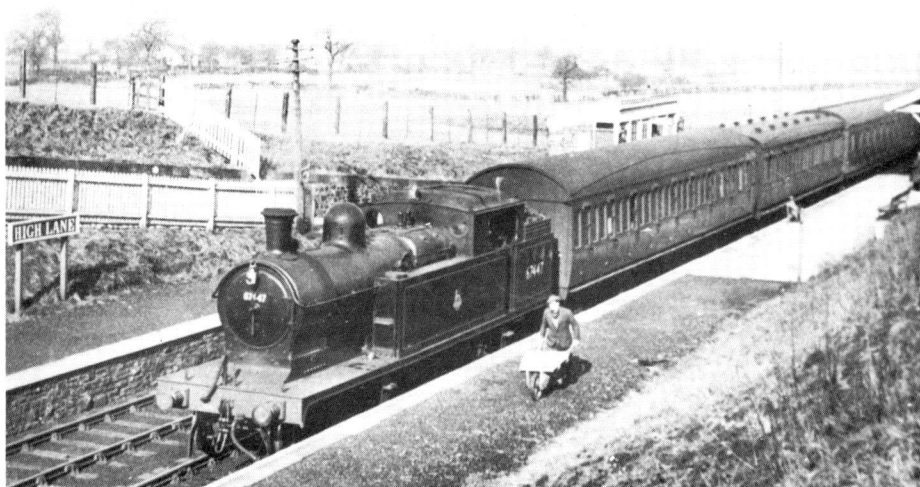

*High Lane just after Nationalisation. Ex G.C. C.14 4.4.2T No 67447 arrives with the 1035 Manchester London Road - Macclesfield Central train on 1st March 1951. Note the small waiting-cum-booking hall on the Down platform. (R. Gee)*

buildings. The girder overbridge which carried the Macclesfield line straddles the station; it now merely serves as a gigantic footbridge linking the station's two platforms, and providing access to each from the many footpaths. However examination of the western end of the Low Level station will reveal that the access arrangements were once even more complicated. There was, for a start, a footbridge linking the Lower Station's two platforms: this was at the western end. Also there was an additional footbridge paralleling the overbridge carrying the Macclesfield line, as indicated by the remaining disused abutments, which carried a footway from the High Level Down platform to the Low Level Up platform via the ramp, which still give access to the Down platform. There were also steps linking the High Level Up platform, and the Low Level Down platform, now brought back into use after the removal of the Low Level's footbridge.

Of the High Level Station closed in 1960, the truncated remains of the Down platform remained intact until recently, but no trace is now visible except at the southern end, where the footpath from the road turns a right angle, there are the remains of steps up to the platform. Of the Up platform some of the concrete footings of the superstructure are visible. The High Level station house is still standing and inhabited, in fact the only habitation in sight.

Leaving this "Crewe" of the woods follow the course of the closed Macclesfield line south. This will bring you to (32) HIGH LEVEL JUNCTION (SJ 945845). Here diverged the Middlewood Curve (L.N.W. & N.S. Joint) opened in 1885 and intended as an express route to Buxton. The service never prospered and ran erratically in the summer until 1927; the curve was closed completely in 1955. The course of the curve is easy to follow; on the left (west) a gradually rising embankment can be seen. This took one line to a flyover crossing the Buxton L.N.W. line. High hopes for this curve must have been entertained for the provision of such lavish facilities - it is the only "flying junction" on the south side of Manchester. To the right, east of this embankment, is the site of three exchange sidings, the other running line, and sidings serving the brickworks.

*Middlewood Higher Station from the south in 1962, 2 years after closure. The platforms and Up buildings remain intact, but the small shelter on the Down side has been removed. The L.N.W. Buxton line is crossed by the bridge just north of the station (Mowat Collection).*

*Site of the Middlewood Curve from High Level Junction in 1962. Part of the curve, closed in 1955, remains as a siding from Low Level Junction. Middlewood Higher Station is visible in the distance. (Mowat Collection).*

Follow the course of the curve, until you approach the L.N.W. Buxton line at (33) LOW LEVEL JUNCTION (SJ 947847), sometimes known as the Aqueduct Junction, as the 53 yard tunnel under the canal counts as an "aqueduct"! The abutments of the flyover bridge over the L.N.W. line have recently been demolished. Now retrace your steps to High Level Junction. From here the walker should strike east across the derelict brickworks and head for the semi-derelict Pool House Farm, and follow a track from there to the Macclesfield Canal of 1826. Follow the canal to the next road bridge and turn right onto the A6.

The cylist and motorist however, cannot follow this track and should return to the road, and retrace your route back to the A6, and High Lane.

Now follow the A6 until it veers off to the right: a minor road, Carr Brow, carries straight on. Follow this uphill for ½ mile, and towards the top, just after a road joins from the right, there is a footpath on the left, by a house, signposted to Stanley Hall. Leave your vehicle here, as it is impossible to get to the next point of interest by car. Take the footpath, skirting the quarry to the top of the hill: from here there is a magnificent view in all directions, extending into the Pennines, and as far as the Wirral on a clear day. Closer at hand, the Marple - New Mills line can be seen threading through the Goyt Valley, and nearer still can be seen 3 of the ventilation shafts of Disley Tunnel with their accompanying spoil heaps. To reach one, do not cross the golf course, but continue along the quarry, and then skirt the course to reach the access track to the Course Club House. Avoid the Club House, and turn left along the track past Stanley Hall. This gives a good view of the 1st and 2nd shafts from the east, but the track actually passes (34) A VENTILATION SHAFT, 3rd from the east (SJ 967855). This is a massive blue brick structure capped with stone. There were 11 such shafts used in the construction of Disley Tunnel, of which 9 remain in use as ventilation shafts. From the adjoining spoil heap, you can see the 1st, 2nd and 4th shafts clearly all in line. Adjoining are Midland Railway boundary posts (made of old rails with one end flattened out, and letters "M.R." attached) indicating that the shaft and spoil heaps remain in railway ownership.

To reach Strines Station, the walker should follow the track downhill straight into Stanley Hall Wood. On emerging from the wood bear right round the drained pool of an old water powered bleach mill. Bear left up out of the valley past the remains of the mill, and after passing some modern farm buildings turn right down a broad path opposite two stone houses. Follow this path down to the main Strines Road and cross it to enter Station Road opposite.

The cyclist and motorist however, will have to return from the shaft to Carr Brow, and take the first road on the right, Wybersley Road. 1 mile further on along the twisting

*A Liverpool - Sheffield d.m.u. passes through Strines on 3rd April 1966 (J.R. Hillier).*

road you reach the Romper Inn; turn right just beyond it down Hollinswood Lane, and follow this to the main Strines Road. Turn right, and on reaching Strines village at the foot of the hill turn left on the road to the station. Walker, cyclist and motorist will pass (35) STRINES PRINTWORKS (SJ 974866) said shortly to close, which once provided most of the traffic for the station goods yard. You also pass the mill pond, with its fine dovecote. (36) STRINES STATION (SJ 978684) vies with Middlewood for the rustic

*Strines - a typical Midland Railway style small country station, with fine gas lamps, neat stone buildings and a large wooden goods shed, c 1962. (Mowat Collection).*

*The heyday of the Midland Railway c 1910. Compound 4.4.0 No 1011 heads a Down Sunday express towards Manchester near Hague Bar, just north of New Mills. Note Strines Down Distant signal with the horizontal stripe, and New Mills Junction's 2 Home Signals - for loop and main line. (Real Photographs).*

tranquillity of its setting. The station was opened in 1866, lost its goods yard in 1963, and became unstaffed in 1973. Until then it had remained a charming gas-lit country station. Now only bare platforms, with electric lights and stone shelters remain. On the Up, eastern, platform the shelter is on the site of the original wooden waiting shelter; just to the south was the footbridge. Opposite on the Down or western platform the site of the station house and buildings can be made out where the platform broadens. Beyond the Up platform is the site of the goods yard. A large wooden goods shed stood against the platform; the foundations of its walls and of 2 hand cranes can be clearly seen. Across the yard was an additional siding for coal. At the far south of the station, at the end of the Up platform, is the clearly visible site of the signalbox, closed in 1980.

The walker should return down the station approach road, and turn right into the bridleway signposted to Greenclough Farm. Just past the farm, turn left, then right at the drinking trough, to follow the valley, and railway line, past Windybottom Farm to Strawberry Hill. Notice the "Roman Bridge" crossing the Goyt on the left - in fact it is a 17th century pack horse bridge. Eventually you draw near (23) MARPLE GOYT VIADUCT. To get a good view of it, leave the track along the river before reaching the viaduct, and follow the path on the right uphill for a short way; then return to the main track.

To complete Trail 2, turn back to location 23 in Trail and follow Trail 1 from location 23 to 20 (in reverse order). From location 20 follow Trail 1 in the proper order from location 24 to 27 to complete Trail 2 at Marple Station.

The cyclist or motorist, however, should retrace his route from Strines Station, and return along Strines Road for 2 miles towards Marple. Just before entering Marple, near the Limekilns, bear right into Arkwright Road off the main road at a fork junction; take the first right of this, Faywood Drive. You are now on course for Trail 1; you should turn back to Trail 1 at location (17) Beechwood, and follow it through to location (27) from there.